# 52 WEEKS
# WITH JESUS
## DEVOTIONAL

# 52 WEEKS WITH JESUS
## DEVOTIONAL

JAMES MERRITT

**HARVEST HOUSE PUBLISHERS**
EUGENE, OREGON

*Cover photo @ jasoncphoto / Fotolia*

*Cover by Dugan Design Group, Bloomington, Minnesota*

Published in association with the literary agency of Wolgemuth & Associates. Inc.

## 52 WEEKS WITH JESUS DEVOTIONAL

Copyright © 2015 by James Merritt
Published by Harvest House Publishers
Eugene, Oregon 97402
www.harvesthousepublishers.com

ISBN 978-0-7369-6556-9 (hardcover)
ISBN 978-0-7369-6557-6 (eBook)

**Printed in China**

16 17 18 19 20 21 22 23 / RDS-JH / 10 9 8 7 6 5 4 3 2

# Contents

## Section 3: Jesus, the Miracle Worker

## Section 4: Jesus, the Storyteller

## Section 5: Jesus, the Teacher

## Section 6: Jesus, the Helper

## Section 7: Jesus, the Leader

## Section 8: Jesus, the Overcomer

# Experience Jesus in a Fresh Way

few years ago I decided to try an experiment of sorts. I committed myself to 52 weeks of getting to know Jesus Christ more deeply. I had been a Christian since I was a boy, but I wanted something more from my relationship with Christ. So I plunged in. For the next year I studied the four Gospel accounts of Jesus's life, took seriously Jesus's words to his disciples, read books about Jesus, and on Sundays my sermons were all about Jesus.

As I had hoped, it was a transformative year for me. My passion for Jesus deepened, I became more aware of his wonder and majesty, and I grew in my compassion for others. What's more, these changes weren't experienced by me alone. Those in my congregation and within my circle of influence who had joined me in this journey were also changed. As a result, I couldn't help but wonder what would happen if thousands—or even tens of thousands—of others could make this same exciting discovery. So I set pen to paper and wrote *52 Weeks with Jesus: Fall in Love with the One Who Changed Everything*. In that book, I presented some Scriptures about Jesus, offered observations I had discovered during my year with him, and closed with a short prayer and a question to contemplate.

On the pages that follow, you'll find 52 devotions that complement the year-long journey found in *52 Weeks with Jesus.* If you've read that book, my hope is this present book will enhance your year-long walk with Jesus even more. If you picked up this book without having read *52 Weeks with Jesus*, that's okay. I'm sure you'll find these devotions a rewarding experience. Each reading is comprised of a portion from Scripture, a short selection from *52 Weeks with Jesus*, and brief insights to help you incorporate what you've read into your life.

My prayer is that you'll find the next 52 weeks a time of transformation, just as it was for me and the many others who have experienced Jesus in a fresh way by getting to know him better.

May God bless your 52 weeks with Jesus!

## Section 1

# Jesus, the Transformer

Birthdays are not unusual—unless the baby happens to be God. We begin our journey with Jesus at a logical place: his lineage and birth. More than a sweet, syrupy Christmas story, Christ's beginning reveals why he should be important to us and why we are important to him.

*52 Weeks with Jesus*

**1**

# Just Like Us

*Jesus, when he began his ministry, was about
thirty years of age, being the son (as was
supposed) of Joseph, the son of Heli* (Luke 3:23).

Jesus was just like us—born with a past and a history—and we have been made to become like him.
God wants you to be a masterpiece of his grace by
living for his glory and expressing his goodness to
others.

*52 Weeks with Jesus*

Both Matthew's and Luke's gospels give us the family
tree of Jesus. The former traces Jesus's earthly lineage
through Joseph (legally, though not biologically, his
father). Luke gives us Jesus's lineage through Mary.

Like Jesus, each of us has a family tree. We all have a

host of ancestors—some of whom were likely scoundrels, others who were godly believers used by God in their day. If we had the chance, which of us would not enjoy a look back through time to witness the odd assortment of men and women whose DNA we share? No matter what surprises we might find there, God has had his hand in the network of branches and offshoots that is our family tree every step of the way. He's even overseen every disastrous wrong turn our ancestors made and then worked it for his ultimate purposes, including the bringing about of *you* for this day and this age.

You have a divine purpose rooted in God's plan. You were born in such a way as to fit uniquely and by design into a great purpose shared by no other human being—past, present, or future.

God's plans always involve people. Ordinary people through whom he can showcase his grace and mercy. Though God has used some of your ancestors in the past— just as he used Abraham, Isaac, David, and others in Jesus's past—he is no longer able to work through them. For now, at this time in history, God can use only *you*.

It is no small thing to be used as a masterpiece of God's grace. Never forget that.

## 2

# A Misfit Among Misfits

*The book of the genealogy of Jesus Christ,
the son of David, the son of Abraham.
Abraham was the father of Isaac, and Isaac
the father of Jacob, and Jacob the father of
Judah and his brothers* (Matthew 1:1-2).

Through Jesus's family tree, God puts his grace on display. God is reminding us that he can do for us what we cannot do for ourselves: pick up broken pieces and put them together, take broken lives and make them whole, gather broken hopes and make them reality. That is the message of Jesus's family tree.

*52 Weeks with Jesus*

Among Jesus's earthly ancestors we find rogues, liars, cheats, prostitutes—every kind of disreputable character imaginable. Then there are the names we usually skip over in the genealogy: Asaph, Abiud, Zadok, Matthan, and many other unnotables. Who were these men? Why are they worthy to be listed in the lineage of the Son of God? And why the Hall of Shame? Where are the royal names in the King of king's lineage? And the ones who lived mostly righteous lives?

There was the great Bible hero David. Oh, but wait— David was an adulterer and murderer. What about Jacob? Ah, yes, he was the deceiver. Rahab? Wasn't she the harlot? And Tamar, the Canaanite; what about her? How ironic that the sinless One—the Redeemer of mankind's sins—should have in his earthly lineage such a roster of sinners themselves. But then what better way to demonstrate that no one is beyond God's grace...beyond God's usefulness?

Rahab no doubt faced a bleak future as the "madam of Jericho." What good thing could she do for the living God of the Israelites? And yet she would choose to betray her warmongering countrymen to become one of God's people. Even more astonishing? She is right there in the puzzling lineup of Jesus's earthly ancestors.

The man who would become King David began as a mere shepherd boy, and son of Jesse. There's not much raw material for a future king in simply herding sheep. Or is there?

The great lesson is, of course, that our past cannot present a stumbling block to God's desire to use us. No matter what we've done, or where we've been, or who we've known, God can still use us...and *will* use us. Using repentant sinners is what God does best.

## 3

# A Messy Messiah

*While the Pharisees were gathered together,*
*Jesus asked them a question, saying, "What*
*do you think about the Christ? Whose*
*son is he?"* (Matthew 22:41-42).

The New Testament is the story of a family: the family of Jesus. God became a part of our family so that we could become a part of his. And just as God used two ordinary women named Ruth and Mary to make a lasting impact on the world, God can use you to make a lasting impression on others by your living for him and loving him and doing his will.

*52 Weeks with Jesus*

Experts say that virtually 100 percent of us are descended from one royal person or another. That each person can be part of a royal family on earth sounds impressive...until we realize that death is the great equalizer. Royal blood counts for nothing when it comes to being part of *God's* royal family. Riches, wealth, and worldly honor will not gain us one square inch of heaven.

The good news is that the blood that gains us acceptance in God's family is the blood of an innocent, slain Lamb of God. Through the death of Christ—and his resurrection—God has opened the doors to the greatest palace of them all...a heavenly home for all who come to him in faith. There we dwell not in the presence of just *a* king, but *the* King of kings.

Many in the Jewish community in Jesus's day didn't recognize their messiah. He wasn't what they expected a messiah to look and act like. Not only were there unsavory characters in his lineage, but there were also Gentiles. *Women* Gentiles at that. Tamar was a Canaanite; Rahab was an Amorite; and Ruth was a Moabitess. But in God's design, none of that mattered.

We all get into the human family—the "Adam" family—the same way Jesus did: by physical, biological birth. However, when it comes to God's family—the Jesus family—we have to be reborn spiritually. By being "born again," we enter into a new family altogether. In this new family, we are invited to make a lasting impact on others as we live for Christ daily.

May we always remember we are, like Adam, only dust. But also, like Christ, we are sons of God and co-heirs of a grand kingdom.

*Christ the Son of God*
*Became a son of Adam*
*That we, sons of Adam,*
*Might become sons of God.*

## Section 2

# Jesus, the Answer

Like Hansel and Gretel, Jesus drops bread crumbs along the path to knowing him. He offers us symbols, images, pictures, and clues to remind us that he is more than skin and bones. Though he is human, he is not like your next-door neighbor or cranky landlord. He is far different—better—than they. Jesus uses seven "I Am" statements in the Gospel of John to share the intricate folds of his personality and identity. They help us understand not only *who* he is but also *what* he wants to be for us.

*52 Weeks with Jesus*

# 4

# Bread for the Journey

*[Jesus said,] "I am the bread*
*of life"* (John 6:35).

After World War II, Europe was overwhelmed with a number of hungry, homeless children who had been orphaned by the conflict. These children were placed in large camps where they received sufficient food and care. But the caregivers noticed the children did not sleep well at night. They were anxious and fearful and restless.

The caregivers were stumped until a psychologist formulated a solution. He instructed the caregivers to give each child a piece of bread, not to eat, but to hold after they were put to bed.

The results astounded all. The children slept through the night because they knew they would have food the next day. Holding bread gave them a sense of security (they were safe), significance (somebody cared about them), and satisfaction (there will be more bread tomorrow). Those things are what those children needed—and what every person needs.

We are all born with this hunger, but our growling souls can be satisfied only by the Bread of Life.

*52 Weeks with Jesus*

We all crave a form of security. Like the orphans of World War II, we want to know we're safe, that someone cares about us, and that somebody will be there for us tomorrow. As Christians, we know that Someone is our heavenly Father. While we sleep, we hold no piece of bread and yet we sleep soundly in his care. We awake each morning knowing the day ahead is filled with the true Bread of life. We need not hunger, nor fear, nor feel unloved. We need only to partake of our daily Bread of life.

**5**

# Light in a Dark Place

*Jesus spoke to them, saying, "I am the
light of the world. Whoever follows
me will not walk in darkness, but will
have the light of life"* (John 8:12).

Light is useful only when it encounters the darkness. The place to shine your light and show your light and share your light is not *inside* the church, but *outside* the church. Jesus tells us to do what he did: go find dark places and start shining.

When you're in the darkness, Jesus shines his light. But if you are living in the light, Jesus calls you to shine into the darkness.

*52 Weeks with Jesus*

There are two kinds of light: true light and reflected light. The sun is true light shining forth from its own power. The moon, on the other hand, is reflected light. It has no light of its own. What we see when we gaze at the bright moon on a clear night is really just a dark orb hanging in space reflecting the light of the sun.

Though we are light, we too are reflected light. When our light shines in the darkness, it's not because we've generated light. Aimed toward the Son of God, we merely reflect his light. When others see our light shining in the darkness of this present world, we can confidently assure them of the true source of our light—Jesus Christ. And we can invite them to join us as reflectors of the true light of the world.

## 6

# An Open Door

*[Jesus said,] "I am the door"* (John 10:9).

People go through life trying to find the doors of security, significance, and satisfaction, but they never do. Be honest with yourself. Are you secure in who you are, what you have, where you are going? Do you feel significant? Are you giving your life to things that matter and make a difference? Are you satisfied? Is there a settled peace in your heart when you go to bed and rise in the morning?

If you are honest and transparent enough to respond no, here are four words Jesus said that you need to hear: "I am the door" (John 10:9).

*52 Weeks with Jesus*

What do you need right now? Peace? Significance? To know you're loved? No matter what your need is, the fulfillment of that need is just beyond the threshold of an open door. You need only to walk through the door that is Christ, and your need will be met—met fully in the One who beckons you to cross the threshold into satisfaction. How do you cross that threshold? You take a step forward...a step of faith. You believe, move ahead, and receive.

## 7

# The Good Life

*[Jesus said,] "I am the good shepherd. I know my own and my own know me, just as the Father knows me and I know the Father; and I lay down my life for the sheep"* (John 10:14-15).

In the first century, a shepherd who embarked on a long journey with a flock of sheep was considered successful if he arrived with more than 50 percent of the flock. That world was full of dangers: disease, poisoned grass, bad water, wild animals. But that is why Jesus is a one-of-a-kind shepherd. When Jesus starts out with a hundred sheep, he ends up with a hundred. He doesn't lose any.

You don't have to live an aimless, helpless life of wandering. Jesus invites you to make him the Good Shepherd in your life and become part of his flock. The good life awaits.

*52 Weeks with Jesus*

The first century shepherd who began a journey with a flock of sheep met many obstacles along the way, some of which could prove fatal to his charges. We twenty-first century sheep are likewise on a long trek. Our journey too is filled with dangers along the way: health issues, troubled relationships, famine, the threat of nuclear destruction. And yet, through all this we have a Good Shepherd who knows the pathway ahead. He knows each bump in the road, each sharp turn, each valley or mountain—and he will bring us through safely. We will only falter when we take our eyes off the Shepherd and look through eyes of fear at the troubles surrounding us. The good life happens only when we turn our eyes back to our Shepherd and follow his steps closely.

# 8

# A Grave Buster

*[Jesus said,] "This sickness will not end in death.
No, it is for God's glory so that God's Son may
be glorified through it"* (John 11:4 NIV).

There are five words in there that not only tell us
why Jesus waits, they tell us why he does *everything*. He says that Lazarus's sickness "will not end
in death" (John 11:4 NIV).

Wait a minute, you may protest, it *did* end in death.
No, Lazarus's sickness *led* to death, but it did not
*end* in death. It *ended* in the glory of God because
Jesus planned to resurrect his adopted brother.

If you are a believer in Jesus Christ, your life is not
going to end in death either. It will *lead* to death,
but because you have eternal life, it *ends* in the glory
of God.

Whatever Jesus is doing in your life, he's doing it
not primarily to satisfy you but to glorify God.
The glory of God is the trump card in the deck of

life—it will always trump our desires, wants, and preferences.

*52 Weeks with Jesus*

Sometimes life is hard. We know God is always at work in us, but our circumstances often leave us scratching our heads. What is God up to with *this* awful situation? Why me, God? Not now, Lord…maybe later. Mary and Martha no doubt asked those questions when their brother, Lazarus, died. After all, death is the ultimate adverse circumstance…or is it? In the story of Lazarus, we find that even in death God has the final say. God's glory will be revealed in the death of *every* believer in Christ. Until then, can we trust him with our present life? Can we allow him to glorify himself today…and tomorrow…and the next day—until our final day when we enter into the glory of heaven?

# 9

# A One-Way Street

*[Jesus said,] "I am the way, and the truth, and the life. No one comes to the Father except through me"* (John 14:6).

▸▸▸▸▸

Over the years I've asked thousands of people, "If you were to stand before God and he were to ask, 'Why should I let you into heaven?' what would you say?" Perhaps this is a dated way of phrasing the question, but the responses I've received reveal something universal:

- "I've always tried to be a good person."
- "I've never [insert abominable sin here]."
- "I try to live a good life."

As I reflect on those answers, I realize many people think getting to God is like going to Home Depot. Almost everyone who is in Home Depot has a project they're trying to do on their own. They want to demolish it themselves, repair it themselves, and build it themselves.

They think you have to build your own highway to God. *I can do this myself. I can be good enough. I can be nice enough. I can donate enough. I can work hard enough.* So the orange cones come out and construction begins.

But Jesus tells us that the highway to God is a *freeway*. No toll is required to get on it, and this freeway has already been built and paid for. Anybody can enter anytime they wish.

*52 Weeks with Jesus*

On the day of our salvation it was like we entered the on-ramp to the freeway of true life—God's freeway. For some of us, we searched for the on-ramp for years. Perhaps in our search we tried various wrong on-ramps that led us down many a dead-end street. Or maybe we tried to fashion our own on-ramp out of the concrete slabs of a broken life...or with the stones that life threw at us. And all the while, God's on-ramp was there...just waiting for us. No toll. No broken slabs. Nothing but a lit-up, green highway sign over the on-ramp that says in bright letters: "This way to heaven."

Until that time, the secret to a happy life is to stay on the Father's freeway! Avoid detours!

## 10

# The Root of the Fruit

*[Jesus said,] "I am the true vine, and my
Father is the vinedresser. Every branch in me
that does not bear fruit he takes away, and
every branch that does bear fruit he prunes,
that it may bear more fruit"* (John 15:1-2).

Jesus's image of the vine illustrates the intimate connection he wants with his followers. This teaching sets Christianity apart from other religions. No other faith offers its followers a personal union with its founder. The Buddhist does not claim to be joined with Buddha. The Confucianist does not claim to be joined to Confucius. The Muslim does not claim to be joined to Mohammed, but Christians claim to be connected to...joined to...Jesus.

This is a point of confusion for many outside the Christian faith. They confuse religion with relationship. They think Christians are following a dead man rather than connecting to a living God.

Following Jesus is not just an *organizational* connection with a church, but an *organic* connection with Christ. Some have done the former rather than the latter, and then they wonder why their faith is fallow and lifeless.

We were created to be organically joined to Christ's life just as branches are connected to a vine.

*52 Weeks with Jesus*

B ranches have no life of their own. In fact, apart from their source of life—the tree or the vine—they're fit for nothing but kindling for the fireplace. But when branches remain connected to their source of life—the vine—much good fruit is born. When our lives lack fruit, there can only be one reason: the life of the vine is no longer flowing through the branches. We have become kindling. At that realization, we must by faith turn away from our self-sufficiency and reconnect with our true vine...and life.

## Section 3

# Jesus, the Miracle Worker

—▸—▸—▸—

Jesus was the greatest wonder-worker who ever lived. He calmed a sea after a storm whipped it into a frenzy. He walked on water, and transformed it into wine. Jesus fed thousands with the equivalent of a Happy Meal and never met a disease he couldn't heal. But these miracles are more than magic tricks. They reveal surprising truths about who Jesus is and spiritual lessons about how we can know and relate to him.

*52 Weeks with Jesus*

# A Man of Marvels

*[Jesus said,] "If I am not doing the works
of my Father, then do not believe me; but if
I do them, even though you do not believe
me, believe the works, that you may know
and understand that the Father is in me and
I am in the Father"* (John 10:37-38).

Here's my working definition for "miracles": *Acts
of God that use or exceed the laws of nature to perform humanly impossible feats to reveal God's power
and glorify him.*

A miracle assumes God *can* perform miracles and
also that God *does*.

The Smithsonian Institute in Washington dis-
plays a leather-bound book called the Jefferson
Bible. This bound volume was the third president's own version of the Bible that he read every
day until he died. Using a razor, Jefferson had cut
and pasted selected verses from the four Gospels, in

chronological order, and removed every reference to a miracle found in any of them. This is a Gospel that excludes the two central miracles of Christianity: the incarnation and the resurrection. So Jefferson rejected both the God who performs miracles and the miracles performed by God.

But Jesus Christ is defined by the miraculous—from his virgin birth to his sinless life to his resurrection. Two of the four Gospels commence with a miracle that C.S. Lewis called the "Grand Miracle": the incarnation of Jesus Christ, God becoming man. If you believe in the incarnation, then you have no trouble believing in miracles. And if you believe in miracles, you're one step closer to fully knowing the One who changed everything.

*52 Weeks with Jesus*

J esus substantiated his claim to be the Son of God by performing the miraculous. Diseases were healed, the blind were given sight, even the dead were raised. It would have taken a first-century onlooker with a very hard and unbelieving heart to deny the source of Jesus's miracles. That's true today too. Skeptics discount the divinity of

Christ. They laugh at the notion that he was resurrected from the dead. As for the miracles Jesus performed, they were either cases of mass hysteria, lies, or sleight of hand. They were anything but proof of Immanuel, which means "God with us" (Matthew 1:23).

The notion that miracles occur is dangerous for skeptics because miracles change everything. If they are real—and they are—then the skeptic has no recourse but to bow his knee. We who believe are also changed by miracles. First, by the miracle of God visiting this earth in the person of Christ. Then, by the miracle of his death—the innocent paying for the guilty. And then, by the resurrection, of which Paul said we are of people most miserable if there is no resurrection. All three of these particular miracles—apart from the many Christ did while walking this earth—have extreme relevance for each of us. The new birth—the most divine miracle for any human being—is the most astonishing miracle to come from the miracle of Christ himself. Our daily walk with God is our ongoing miracle to enjoy on our way to the grandest miracle—the miracle of eternity with God. The entirety of who we are as Christians rests on the miraculous. We must, therefore, never doubt the power of our miracle-performing God.

## 12

# Crisis Manager

*[Jesus's mother said,] "Do whatever he tells you"* (John 2:5).

⤚⤚⤚⤚

What a great piece of advice! Jesus never met a problem that he could not solve if the afflicted would only do what he tells them to. Too many of us know what Jesus wants us to do, but we refuse to do it. Jesus said, "If you know these things, blessed are you if you do them" (John 13:17).

Sometimes we assume that obedience follows blessing. And sometimes it does. When God gives to us, we should respond with devotion out of joy. But in this story, the water was not transformed until the jars were filled to the brim the way Jesus requested. Often, blessing follows obedience.

Jesus tells the servants to draw out some of the water and take it to the master of ceremonies to taste. Those jars normally held water that was used to wash dirty hands, not wine for a wedding. These men could have been sent to prison for such a disgraceful act. But they obeyed anyway.

Their obedience *to* Jesus led to great blessing *from* Jesus. So it is with our lives.

*52 Weeks with Jesus*

————

Daily obedience to Christ yields daily blessings from Christ. What we sow, we reap. If we sow disobedience, we can't complain when our disobedience brings us an unwanted harvest of pain and sorrow. If we sow obedience—if we simply do what we know we should— we find blessing. Oh yes, there may still be pain. Life is like that. But the richest blessing from obedience is the peace of God that keeps us upright during any winds of affliction that blow our way.

"Trust and obey," the old hymn rightly says. "Trust and obey, for there's no other way to be happy in Jesus, but to trust and obey."

## 13

# Captain of My Ship

*Leaving the crowd, they took him with them in the boat, just as he was. And other boats were with him. And a great windstorm arose, and the waves were breaking into the boat, so that the boat was already filling. But he was in the stern, asleep on the cushion. And they woke him and said to him, "Teacher, do you not care that we are perishing?" And he awoke and rebuked the wind and said to the sea, "Peace! Be still!" And the wind ceased, and there was a great calm. He said to them, "Why are you so afraid? Have you still no faith?" And they were filled with great fear and said to one another, "Who then is this, that even the wind and the sea obey him?"* (Mark 4:36-41).

It may sound shocking, but *we need storms*. Christ allows us to sail into them so we'll remember his promises, rest in his presence, and rely on his power.

I don't know what storm you are going through right now, what storm you are coming out of, or what storm you may be heading into. But Jesus wants you to turn your face toward him and remember that there is no need to fear when he is near. That's why he wants to be the Captain of your life's ship.

*52 Weeks with Jesus*

The disciples—some of whom were fishermen—were caught up short when an obviously unexpected storm arose. The very men who fished these waters were afraid of perishing. If only they'd realized who was sleeping soundly through the storm in the stern of their boat! They would have understood then how foolish it was to worry. But, really, are we any wiser? When an unexpected storm brings dark clouds, sharp winds, and pouring rain into our lives, do we not fear just as the disciples did?

This very unexpected storm had a great purpose, though. It turned out to be an opportunity to learn the lesson that, yes, Jesus has power over storms.

If you're in a storm now—particularly an unexpected

storm—remember who's in the boat with you. He will calm the tempest after it has served its purpose. Jesus will soon say, "Peace! Be still!" to the turbulent winds in your life, and they will cease. In the meantime, consider the question Jesus asked of the disciples: "Have you still no faith?" Let your answer be, "Lord, I do believe. Help my unbelief during the raging storm."

# 14

# A Miraculous Multiplier

*Jesus said, "Have the people sit down." Now
there was much grass in the place. So the men
sat down, about five thousand in number.
Jesus then took the loaves, and when he had
given thanks, he distributed them to those who
were seated. So also the fish, as much as they
wanted. And when they had eaten their fill,
he told his disciples, "Gather up the leftover
fragments, that nothing may be lost." So they
gathered them up and filled twelve baskets
with fragments from the five barley loaves left
by those who had eaten* (John 6:10-13).

When Jesus asks the disciples to have everyone sit
down for supper, I imagine a few wanted to call a
psychiatrist. But then Jesus does something outra-
geous. He gives thanks! Why was Jesus grateful for a
tiny meal that could barely feed a child in the midst
of a hungry crowd?

This is how God operates: Jesus asks for what he desires. We give to Jesus what he asks. Jesus uses what we give. Even the smallest gifts.

God has a habit of using little things to accomplish unbelievable things: a shepherd boy's slingshot, the change in a widow's purse, a poverty-stricken teenage virgin, and seed-sized faith.

Do you know what determines something's value? The one whose hands it's put into. You can buy a professional baseball online for about twelve dollars. If you put it into the hands of a major-league pitcher, it is worth millions. In the same way, what made that little boy's lunch so valuable was not its size but his willingness to offer it to Jesus.

Anything you have is valuable if you are willing to give it to Christ.

*52 Weeks with Jesus*

Sometimes we think we have nothing of value to offer the Lord. Our natural talents are meager at best. Our attempts to come alongside others in pain seem awkward. We're aware of how very little we have to give. But then aren't we looking at the baseball as it remains in our human hands? The lesson of Scripture is that the size of the gift isn't what matters, it's in whose hands the gift is placed.

When we look around and see how used of God others seem to be, we're reminded of our own inadequacy. But that's not how God views the situation at all. God sees our seemingly small gifts through the magnifying lens of his power—power that enlarges every gift to perfectly fit the present need. Someday, in eternity perhaps, we'll meet the little boy who made his insignificant lunch available to the Master. I'm sure he'll have much to say about God's willingness to use our small offerings to his service.

# 15

# A Leader Worth Following

*Jesus said to them, "Follow me, and I will*
*make you become fishers of men"* (Mark 1:17).

━━━━━

From the time we were born, the first lesson Jesus
wanted us to learn was not how to lead but how to
follow. The first lesson Jesus wants you to learn is
not how to be over but how to be under.

*52 Weeks with Jesus*

━━━━━

Isn't it striking that Jesus could choose twelve men to follow him who wouldn't argue with him? Who wouldn't
say, "No, Jesus, let's do it *my* way this time"? Oh sure,
from time to time they questioned Jesus's decisions. They
even argued over which of them should sit at his right hand
when he's ruling his kingdom. But the disciples somehow
knew they were there to *follow* him, not to lead him.

How often do we say, "No, Lord—let's do it my way this time"? And yet when we stop trying to manipulate God to our way of doing something and let him lead, we find that he was right all along.

When God makes a decision regarding our lives, it's always the right decision. Why? Because he's the leader, and we are the followers. There is such contentment in that, isn't there?

# 16

# The Great Empathizer

*Jesus said to the paralyzed man, "My child,
your sins are forgiven"* (Mark 2:5 NLT).

––––

Christianity is the only spiritual philosophy that
addresses our greatest problem, which is sin, and
meets our greatest need, which is forgiveness. If my
sins have been forgiven, if my place is secured in
heaven, if I no longer have to fear death, then I can
face anything else. When I can stand before a holy
and righteous God and declare that because of the
cross my sins are forgiven, Jesus gets excited.

*52 Weeks with Jesus*

––––

Was Adam's disobedience in Eden *really* that
awful? Is our own disobedience (whether
through our ignorance or through deliberation)

such a big deal? To answer that question, we have only to look at God's remedy for sin. It was nothing less than the death of his Son at the hands of angry sinners, who are a fair representation of us.

It was, as we know, the exchange of the innocent (Jesus) for the guilty (us). There was no other option for solving the sin issue. None! Either a divine payment would be made, or every person who ever lived would one day stand before God accountable for each and every sinful act they committed.

Instead, through God's great mercy and Jesus's divine payment—that *full* payment—we will someday stand guiltless before God and reap an eternal inheritance laid up for us that we don't deserve.

To be entirely forgiven of our sins is a remarkable thing. To have the innocent Son of God die on our behalf reveals the severity of sin and the depth of God's love for us.

## 17

# The Divine Ophthalmologist

*[Jesus] spit on the ground and made mud with the saliva. Then he anointed the man's eyes with the mud and said to him, "Go, wash in the pool of Siloam" (which means Sent). So he went and washed and came back seeing* (John 9:6-7).

The old adage says, "Seeing is believing." But in this case, believing is seeing.

That this man went and washed as Jesus instructed means that he believed Jesus. If he hadn't, if this man had said, "I don't know why you're doing this. I don't understand it, and until I do, I'm not going to believe it and I'm not going to obey you," he would have died blind.

But he believed Jesus because he was desperate.

Nobody else had offered a cure. Nobody else had offered a change. Nobody else had offered an opportunity for healing.

If you're living a life of quiet desperation, and if you want your place of desperation to become a setting for God's transformation, believe what Jesus says about you. Believe what Jesus says about himself. And believe what Jesus says he can do through you, in you, and for you.

*52 Weeks with Jesus*

Sometimes we're too skeptical for our own good. God calls us to do something by faith, and we respond by looking through our natural eyes at the implications...and ask God for plan B.

Jesus gave sight to a blind man who was willing to do what Jesus told him to do. He didn't weigh the implications of not obeying. He didn't reason as to why Jesus's request would make him look foolish in the eyes of others. There were no theological complications for the man to consider—there was just a fresh chance for a desperate man who had no other options.

"Go, wash in the pool of Siloam," Jesus told the man. The man obeyed, and his sight was given to him. The story gets even better in that the man was also given *spiritual* sight that enabled him to respond to Jesus's question "Do you believe in the Son of Man?" with the eager words, "And who is he, sir, that I may believe in him?" (John 9:35-36).

The blind man earned a place in the Word of God that will never be taken from him. He also learned that obedience to Christ is its own reward.

## 18

# Spiritually Sovereign

*Submit yourselves, then, to God. Resist the devil,*
*and he will flee from you* (James 4:7 NIV).

I've often been asked, "Is it possible for a Christian to be demon-possessed?" The answer to that question is a decisive no. Once the Holy Spirit takes control of a Christian's life, all the demons in hell can't force the Spirit to move out. But followers of Christ can be demon-influenced. That is why we need to keep our spiritual guard up, stay in the Word, continue to pray, and not allow ourselves to fall into temptation...

When you trust Christ as your Savior and God's Spirit comes to live within you, demons will attack you, but they can never possess or defeat you.

*52 Weeks with Jesus*

It seems Christians are easily given to extremes. When it comes to the unpleasant topic of demons, Christians may err on the side of placing too much emphasis on demons or, on the opposite side, by denying their influence entirely—sometimes to the extent of ridiculing the reality of demons ("The devil made me do it. Ha ha ha!").

Serious students of the Bible will recognize and not shy away from the reality of demons and their ability to influence anyone who invites their presence. Christians, however, have nothing to fear when it comes to demons. Christ in us is stronger than *any* demonic influence that may attack us. The secret to maintaining victory over satanic influence of any kind is to heed the apostle James's admonition to a) submit ourselves fully to God and b) resist demonic or satanic influence. When we do those two things, God's Word tells us Satan (and, by extension, his demons) will have to flee.

A careful examination of Jesus's encounters with demons in the New Testament confirms this truth. Demons were terrified of the power Jesus held over them. And the good news is that demons are terrified of the power we twenty-first-century believers have over them too.

Just remember to submit to God and to resist the devil. That formula results in Satan fleeing our presence every single time.

## Section 4

# Jesus, the Storyteller

▸▸▸▸

Spellbinding. Penetrating. Heart-touching. These are fitting adjectives for the stories Jesus told. No less than 35 percent of Jesus's recorded teachings were parables—stories designed to reveal truth— and no one knew how to spin a story better. More than ordinary "once upon a time" tales, Jesus tells earthly stories imbued with both eternal and practical meanings. The stories Jesus told were not for entertainment but for edification; not for information but for transformation. If you want to know who Jesus was and what he valued, take a plunge into the parables he told.

*52 Weeks with Jesus*

## 19

# The Seed Sower

*Then [Jesus] told them many things in parables, saying: "A farmer went out to sow his seed..."* (Matthew 13:3 NIV).

All a farmer can do is sow seed. Once he does, the harvest is in God's hands. Our job is to sow. God's job is to grow. The key to reaching missing people is not the presentation of the message. It is the penetration of the heart. The presentation is our part. The penetration is God's part.

The equation might look something like this:

Faithful Sharers + Fertile Soil = Fruitful Success

Jesus only asks for you to share what you know and live what you share.

You can sow and have no harvest; the parable proves this. But if you don't sow, there will never be a harvest.

One of the things I do at my church is to challenge folks to ask Christ to give them three people that they could plant their lives into—three people into whom they could sow the seed of his Word—trusting Jesus for the harvest...You do your job. Jesus will do his.

*52 Weeks with Jesus*

W hat has God done in your life? Have you been dramatically saved from a hard life of drugs, sexual immorality, and other sins? Or was your conversion less dramatic, though just as real? Perhaps you were brought up in a Christian family and never wandered far from God. Still, you know the Lord has saved you from a lesser life to a greater life—and an eternal inheritance.

When we sow the seed of the gospel to others, the seed is, of course, the Word of God. But you, as the sower, have a different story to tell than the person in the pew next to you on Sunday morning. Every Christian is unique, and thus every conversion is unique. Your story—whether dramatic or seemingly tame—is important. Part of your method of sowing seeds is to give witness to what the Word of God— the seed—has produced in your life.

You may not be called to be an evangelist, but you are called to evangelize, which is simply sowing the seed of God's Word and telling your story. You may find it valuable to write out the effects of the seed of God's Word in your life and rehearse it in private. When God brings a person along to whom you can sow the seed, you'll be ready with a good explanation of how the gospel changes lives. Beyond that, God bears the responsibility to see the seed produce fruit.

## 20

# The Best Boss

*The workers who were hired about five in the afternoon came and each received a denarius. So when those came who were hired first, they expected to receive more. But each one of them also received a denarius. When they received it, they began to grumble against the landowner. "These who were hired last worked only one hour," they said, "and you have made them equal to us who have borne the burden of the work and the heat of the day."*

*But he answered one of them, "I am not being unfair to you, friend. Didn't you agree to work for a denarius? Take your pay and go. I want to give the one who was hired last the same as I gave you. Don't I have the right to do what I want with my own money? Or are you envious because I am generous?"*

*So the last will be first, and the first will be last* (Matthew 20:9-16 NIV).

The man hired at the end of the day came home to his wife and kids and put a denarius down on the table.

His wife hugged him and said, "Thank God you got to work today. We were running out of food and you came through. I know you must be exhausted."

"Not really. I only worked an hour."

The wife looked at him with a puzzled expression. "But that's a full day's wage. How did you get that when you only worked for an hour?"

"Don't ask me. I just know I got hired at five o'clock. I worked one hour. He paid me the same thing he paid the man who came to work at six this morning."

The wife looked at him and said, "You got what you didn't deserve."

With a broad smile on his face, the man said, "Don't we all?"

He seemed to know something about the master's grace, didn't he? After working enough days for stingy bosses, he had finally encountered a master who was gracious and generous.

Look at everything you have. Not just materially
but relationally, socially, financially, and even phys-
ically and realize that it is all just grace.

*52 Weeks with Jesus*

The kingdom of God is very different from kingdoms
on earth. Down here, we look at what others have or
have not, and we compare our lives with theirs. What
really galls us is the guy who inherited more money than
we'll ever make in a lifetime. He spends his days on the golf
course or is off on another exotic vacation. We think of him
often when the alarm goes off at six o'clock in the morning
and we must get ready for work. We're also envious of the
woman at work who was just promoted to supervisor when
she's been with the company for less time than we have. And
what of our neighbor who just won the lottery? We're envious even though we sent what we could have spent on lottery tickets to support that missionary in Peru.

But wait. Aren't we Christians? Don't we belong to
another kingdom not of this world? In this kingdom, we're
happy to see God's grace reach the undeserving. Why?
Because we finally get it. We finally see that we're all undeserving and that the economic policy of heaven comes from

our heavenly Father's attribute of generosity. He's a giver, and we're so blessed to be recipients of his giving that we want others to benefit too.

To see God as the God of grace is to understand that we all are the workers who showed up at the last hour. And aren't we glad we serve such a generous master?

## 21

# The Eye Opener

*"Which of these three do you think was a neighbor to the man who fell into the hands of robbers?"*

*The expert in the law replied, "The one who had mercy on him."*

*Jesus told him, "Go and do likewise"* (Luke 10:36-37 NIV).

⊳⊳⊳

To a first-century Jew, the only good Samaritan was a dead Samaritan. No class or race of people was hated more by the Jewish people than Samaritans. They were publicly cursed in the synagogue and were excluded from temple worship. Prayers would be offered every day begging God to keep them out of heaven.

Why? Pure racism.

[In Jesus's parable of the Good Samaritan,] what this Samaritan does is nothing short of amazing. He uses all his available resources—oil, wine, personal clothing, his animal, time, energy, and money—to give this Jewish man the best care possible.

The Samaritan risks his own life by taking this wounded man to an inn in Jewish territory. Then, to top it off, the Samaritan gives the innkeeper enough money to cover the man's food and lodging for several days, then promises to come back and pay anything else the man owes. This is important, because any person who could not pay their bill could be sold as a slave by the innkeepers in order to get full payment for a debt.

When Jesus asks which man proved to be a good neighbor, the lawyer couldn't even spit out the word Samaritan. Instead, he mumbles, "The one who showed him mercy."

What made this Samaritan so special was not the color of his skin but the compassion in his heart. No law will ever make you be a good neighbor, but real love can't keep you from being a good neighbor.

A neighbor is not defined by color or creed; a neighbor is defined by nearest need.

*52 Weeks with Jesus*

How might the story of the Good Samaritan apply to us? To answer that, we simply have to recall how we've behaved in the past when confronted by a person with a need we were aware of. What was our response? "Well, his church should help him." "The government should step in. That's why I pay taxes." "There are plenty of places he can get help." "I'd like to help, but I'm too busy." I'm sure you can think of more excuses people use.

Though these are the wrong responses, perhaps the worst response is simply refusing to see the need. In a sense, that's what the priest and the Levite did when they saw the injured man but chose to cross the road and pass by on the other side. They distanced themselves from the need. In so doing, they were turning their eyes away. If we don't "see" the need, doesn't that mean we're justified in not stopping to help?

But think for a minute about our own desperate need. We were lost and alienated from God. We were his enemies, robbed, as it were, by Satan's schemes against us. What did God do when he saw our need? Instead of passing by on the other side, instead of pretending not to see us, God stepped in. He intervened big time. He offered what he had—his Son, Jesus—to restore us.

How then can we, who were once robbed and left to die, not stop to render aid to those in need? How can we not cross from our side of the road to theirs and extend hands of mercy?

## 22

# The Divine Auditor

*It will be like a man going on a journey, who called his servants and entrusted to them his property. To one he gave five talents, to another two, to another one, to each according to his ability* (Matthew 25:14-15).

God has given every one of us certain abilities, unique personalities, and personal opportunities that he expects us to leverage for his glory and for the good of others. Just like money, they are to be invested...

All Christ wants every one of us to do is play our part. Jesus does not expect the same results, but he does expect the same effort. He never compares you with anyone else. He compares you only with you. Jesus doesn't look at what you have. He looks only at what you do with what you have.

*52 Weeks with Jesus*

In the parable of the talents, Jesus told the story of a master who entrusted three servants with five, two, and one talent, respectively. When he returned from a trip, he was pleased with the first two servants for having wisely invested the talents. But the master chided the third servant who had buried the talent to keep it safe. In short, the third servant did nothing with what he'd been entrusted.

It didn't matter to the master the amount of talents each was given. What mattered was what each servant did with his portion. So too we are entrusted with a portion of our Master's estate, and we are expected to be profitable (not profitless) servants. What then are we doing with what we've been given? Are we going off alone, figuratively burying what we've been given? Or are we proactively searching for the best place to invest our portion? If we're unsure of how to invest what we've been given, we can pray and we can ask others (including church leadership) how they suggest we use our gifts to further God's kingdom. We can also respond to providential circumstances that may reveal our gifts. God doesn't hide his gifts to us from us. He makes them evident, and He looks for returns on his investments.

# 23

# A Better Financial Planner

*[Jesus] said to them, "Take care, and be on your guard against all covetousness, for one's life does not consist in the abundance of his possessions."...And he told them a parable, saying, "The land of a rich man produced plentifully, and he thought to himself, 'What shall I do, for I have nowhere to store my crops?'"* (Luke 12:15-17).

━━━━▶

Covetousness is one sin you can keep a secret and nobody notices. You could be a covetous person twenty-four hours a day and nobody but you would ever know it...

Most people think that what they have is for them. But if you understand that everything you have comes from [God] and is for him, you will handle your finances completely differently...

The only cure for covetousness, the only solution for selfishness, and the only medicine for materialism is giving to those who need what you have by becoming rich toward God. That is what Jesus did for us by dying for our sins, and that is what we can do for others in turn. If Jesus were a rich man, that is what he would do.

*52 Weeks with Jesus*

ovetousness is a secret offense. Not only can others not see it, often we can't see it in ourselves. We're just admiring that new Corvette our neighbor bought, we tell ourselves. We're just complimenting our friend on her good taste in clothes. We're just congratulating our coworker who got the promotion we'd hoped for.

But when we're finally ready to concede that we do covet, God has the remedy—the wake-up call that reminds us our lives don't draw value from the abundance of our possessions. Everything we have comes from God, and everything we have is for him.

To be emotionally detached from our possessions is a great freedom that few enjoy. Just remember: What good thing do you have that hasn't come to you through the benevolence of God? How, then, can you claim it as your own?

# 24

# The God of Tomorrow

*The love of money is a root of all kinds of evils. It is through this craving that some have wandered away from the faith and pierced themselves with many pangs* (1 Timothy 6:10).

One day, everything you have or think you have will be gone. It will either be lost somehow before you die, or certainly gone after you die. One day you are going to lose it, so use it today to get ready for tomorrow.

That is exactly what Jesus did when he died on the cross and was raised from the dead. He invested the life that he lived those thirty-three years on earth, so we could get ready for the tomorrow of eternity.

Take everything you have, everything you are, and give it to Christ today so you will be ready for tomorrow.

*52 Weeks with Jesus*

J esus taught more about money than any other topic. That's astonishing, really. But perhaps not so much when we consider our love of money. This misplaced love was also a fault of the Pharisees who ridiculed Jesus when he spoke of money issues through parables. Paul tells us that the love of money has caused some believers to wander away from their faith. The result? They "pierced themselves with many pangs."

Money is like sand sifting through our fingers. If we try to close our fist rather than relax it, we'll gather no more. But if we allow money to pass on to others in need, God will supply more, in keeping with what he chooses to entrust us with. We don't want to make the acquisition of money our goal. It brings us nothing of eternal value, and it brings pain and conflict during this earthly life.

# 25

# The Life of the Party

*[Jesus said,] "I tell you, there will be more joy in heaven over one sinner who repents than over ninety-nine righteous persons who need no repentance"* (Luke 15:7).

━━━►►►

Every time one person repents, every time one person surrenders their life to Jesus Christ, every time one lost person is found, God says, "It's party time!"

Can you imagine the angels up in heaven as they gaze upon God? All of a sudden God begins to shout, dance, and rejoice. He breaks out the food and the drink. One angel says, "There he goes again. Somebody else just repented. Somebody else just got found. Somebody else just surrendered to Jesus."

Because lost people matter to Jesus, they matter to us. And as we pursue the lost with the love of Christ, heaven rejoices.

*52 Weeks with Jesus*

J esus had just told the story of the good shepherd who left ninety-nine sheep to search for one lost lamb. After finding the wandering one, the shepherd rejoiced and threw a party. So it is in heaven when one lost person finds Christ. There is great rejoicing among the angels.

Do we value the lost around us enough to care for them as Jesus cares for them? We surely would if we fully grasped the value God places on a lost person. That value is the life of his Son. If only we could hear the party going on in heaven—we would surely join in with great abandon.

# 26

# Hospitable Host

*The master said to the servant, "Go out to the highways and hedges and compel people to come in, that my house may be filled. For I tell you, none of those men who were invited shall taste my banquet"* (Luke 14:23-24).

⸺⸺⸺⸺

Once when former president George H.W. Bush was in Atlanta, I was invited to bring my sons to a fund-raising dinner for a candidate who was running for election. I was told we would be sitting at the table with the former president.

I didn't say, "I wish I could, but I must go to Kroger's and shop."

I didn't even say, "Sorry, but I've got a golf match that day."

I said, "I'll be there."

I received that invitation. I honored that invitation. I heeded that invitation. Now my sons and I have a memory we will never forget.

We've all been given a far greater invitation to sit at the table of the Creator of the universe, the King of kings and the Lord of lords, and to enjoy his presence forever.

*52 Weeks with Jesus*

Eternity in heaven with God will be bliss. There will be a special dinner—the wedding supper of the Lamb—to which we are invited. But the time to accept the invitation is not then, but now. Will we come? Will we accept the host's divine invitation? If we say yes, the good news is that our heavenly bliss can begin now. The invitation God offers everyone is joy here while we await that great day and then final everlasting joy at the wedding banquet. What invitation on earth can possibly compare with God's party? Will you RSVP?

# 27

# The Object of Our Worship

*Two men went up to the temple to pray, one
a Pharisee and the other a tax collector. The
Pharisee stood by himself and prayed: "God,
I thank you that I am not like other people—
robbers, evildoers, adulterers—or even like this
tax collector. I fast twice a week and give a tenth
of all I get."*

*But the tax collector stood at a distance. He
would not even look up to heaven, but beat his
breast and said, "God, have mercy on me, a
sinner."*

*I tell you that this man, rather than the other,
went home justified before God. For all those
who exalt themselves will be humbled, and
those who humble themselves will be exalted*
(Luke 18:10-14 NIV).

One man in Jesus's story was rejected by God and the other was accepted. Why? Because of how they looked at themselves...You will see yourself correctly only when you see God correctly. When you see God correctly you will understand that only God is perfect and no one else is.

*52 Weeks with Jesus*

The mark of a Pharisee today is that he or she has a remarkably righteous exterior. A Pharisee never partakes of the sinful activities that his unrighteous neighbor is involved in. But if we could see the interior of both the Pharisee and the sinner, we might come to a more accurate conclusion that the Pharisee has a corrupt heart hidden behind that religious facade. We might see that the sinner has a heart for God but has been entrapped by sin for so long that he or she finds it hard to be set free. All that sinner can do is cry out to God for mercy. The good news is that God hears prayers like that and grants mercy to the sinner. May we always be counted among the sinners crying for mercy and not the Pharisees clamoring to be noticed for righteous acts.

## 28

# The Grace Giver

*The older son was in the field. When he came near the house, he heard music and dancing. So he called one of the servants and asked him what was going on. "Your brother has come," he replied, "and your father has killed the fattened calf because he has him back safe and sound."*

*The older brother became angry and refused to go in. So his father went out and pleaded with him. But he answered his father, "Look! All these years I've been slaving for you and never disobeyed your orders. Yet you never gave me even a young goat so I could celebrate with my friends. But when this son of yours who has squandered your property with prostitutes comes home, you kill the fattened calf for him!"*

*"My son," the father said, "you are always with me, and everything I have is yours. But we had to celebrate and be glad, because this brother of yours was dead and is alive again; he was lost and is found"* (Luke 15:25-32 NIV).

Do you know why a lot of younger brothers are still out there in the pigpen and don't want to come into the church? They see a church full of older brothers who don't want them to come and are afraid if they do come, they will be slapped with the cold hand of judgment rather than touched with the warm hand of love.

Self-righteous people think that unrighteous people can never be forgiven and should never be forgiven. But while the older brother is into punishment, the father is into pardon. The older brother is into guilt, but the father is into grace. The older brother is into revenge, but the father is into reconciliation.

No matter how far you've wandered, no matter how low you've sunk, know that upon your return, you will find the Father in front of an open door with open arms and a loving heart.

There is one door that is always open, and that is the door to the Father's house.

*52 Weeks with Jesus*

There's a little of the older brother in most of us. Perhaps we've served the Lord faithfully with little recognition…and then along comes this "younger brother" in the form of a new Christian, or a returning backslider, or the owner of the local adult bookstore who has just repented, closed his business, and is giving his testimony to great acclaim all over town.

The younger brother's wake-up call had been when he was at his worst—destitute, hungry, *lost*. But this story has a wake-up call for the older brother as well. The father reminds his angry boy, "My son…you are always with me, and everything I have is yours." In short, in this story everyone wins—but we need to set aside our jealousy and resentment to join our returning younger brother in the festivities. After all, the door to the Father's house that is always open, is always open to the older brother as well. Only our wrong attitude keeps us from stepping through it.

## 29

# Discerner of the Heart

*Jesus told them another parable: "The kingdom of heaven is like a man who sowed good seed in his field. But while everyone was sleeping, his enemy came and sowed weeds among the wheat, and went away. When the wheat sprouted and formed heads, then the weeds also appeared.*

*"The owner's servants came to him and said, 'Sir, didn't you sow good seed in your field? Where then did the weeds come from?'*

*"'An enemy did this,' he replied.*

*"The servants asked him, 'Do you want us to go and pull them up?'*

*"'No,' he answered, 'because while you are pulling the weeds, you may uproot the wheat with them. Let both grow together until the harvest. At that time I will tell the harvesters: First collect the weeds and tie them in bundles to be burned; then gather the wheat and bring it into my barn'"* (Matthew 13:24-30 NIV).

Are you a weed or are you wheat?

Whether you are a Baptist or a Catholic, baptized or not, religious or nonreligious, a church member or not, it is all irrelevant. The question that matters is this: Are you a weed or are you wheat? And the answer can be gleaned from one other question: Who is your Father? That alone will determine where you spend eternity.

For two thousand years the Lord has been sowing generation after generation of his saints into the world. They are scattered everywhere. They take root, flourish, bear fruit, and give witness to the fact that God is at work all over the world.

Yet, in a spiritual sense, all wheat stalks begin as weeds. There was a time when you and I were not wheat; we were weeds. There was a time when you and I were not saints; we were sinners. We needed a Savior who could turn us into saints.

Turning a sinner into a saint is something only God can do.

*52 Weeks with Jesus*

So often we try to cultivate ourselves. It's as if we believe we can make ourselves grow stronger spiritually, as if we could turn ourselves from weeds into wheat. We can't. How we grow is a direct result of who our Father is. If God is our Father, as we claim, then he alone will grow us. He has, in fact, saved us so he can grow us into mature stalks of the finest wheat.

The reason for God's tender care, of course, is that as we grow we can never claim credit for the results and the fruit he produces through us. When God is the grower, God gets the credit. If we are truly wheat, we have come to know this through our own failed attempts of trying to act like wheat. When we rest and trust God, we no longer need to act. We simply *are* wheat.

## 30

# A Divine Divider

*[The rich man] answered, "Then I beg you,
father, send Lazarus to my family, for I have
five brothers. Let him warn them, so that they
will not also come to this place of torment."*

*Abraham replied, "They have Moses and the
Prophets; let them listen to them."*

*"No, father Abraham," he said, "but if someone
from the dead goes to them, they will repent."*

*He said to him, "If they do not listen to Moses
and the Prophets, they will not be convinced
even if someone rises from the dead"* (Luke
16:27-31 NIV)

Nobody gets to determine how they enter this
world. You didn't get to determine the place of your
birth, the time of your birth, or even the color of
your skin. What we do get to determine is how we

leave this world. You didn't get to determine your entrance. You do get to determine your exit.

But you don't make that decision at the moment you breathe your final breath. Rather, today's decision determines tomorrow's destiny...Begin now to live for God, look to God, and listen to God, for that is the only life that will matter both today and tomorrow.

*52 Weeks with Jesus*

—————

Do you fear death? My 93-year-old mother said she didn't fear death itself, just the fact that it was the unknown. As she said, "You only do it once, so you don't get to practice." Mom was right, but in more ways than she realized. Not only do we pass through death once, so too do we only pass through life once. We don't get to practice life. What we're living today is not a dress rehearsal...it *is* our life. Each day we live we're busy making choices that lead to our destiny. Is that destiny propelling us toward an eternity where we might have Lazarus as a next door neighbor? Or is our destiny with the rich man in torment who thought only of today and never of eternity?

Living the kind of life that produces the right destiny isn't hard, though, like Lazarus, we may experience pain and deprivation. What's really hard is living for this world only. The rich man dressed himself in purple as a sign of his great wealth. But even in a purple shroud, his destiny was to be with the poorest of the poor—those separated from God. That's the true poverty of the universe.

## Section 5

# Jesus, the Teacher

▸▸▸▸

Scholars debate almost everything about who Jesus was and what he did. But all agree he was a masterful teacher. He spoke with an understanding of spirituality and philosophical depth that continues to dazzle the minds of the masses. His teaching addresses life's most pressing problems and helps us navigate through them. The trick is to encounter Jesus's familiar phrases and well-trod wisdom with fresh eyes.

*52 Weeks with Jesus*

## 31

# Flying Standby

*Why do you look at the speck of sawdust in your brother's eye and pay no attention to the plank in your own eye? How can you say to your brother, "Let me take the speck out of your eye," when all the time there is a plank in your own eye? You hypocrite, first take the plank out of your own eye, and then you will see clearly to remove the speck from your brother's eye* (Matthew 7:3-5 NIV).

If you want to see what you look like, you look in a mirror. If you want to see what someone else looks like, you look out a window. Jesus is saying we need to spend more time looking in the mirror and less time looking out the window. The next time you see a splinter in someone else's life, look for the log that is in your own. Remember, the splinter is just a piece of the log. What you see in others is just a reflection of what you see in you.

*52 Weeks with Jesus*

ave you ever caught yourself mentally criticizing someone else and immediately you remembered that very fault you're seeing in someone else is similar to a failing in your own life? Or perhaps you're ready to judge someone when you suddenly realize they're dealing with a sin you once had to overcome. Just as you're ready to mentally pounce on them, you stop and pray: *"Oh, Lord! That was me not so very long ago. How could I have forgotten what it's like so easily?"*

God saves us all for a reason. Part of his plan is for those of us who have found freedom from a particular sin to walk alongside and befriend those still struggling. That's 180 degrees from our natural inclination to cluck our tongues in judgment.

It may also be out of our comfort zone to come alongside someone who is wrestling with fierce temptations. But when we allow compassion to move us to action, we imitate Christ's actions on our behalf.

So whenever you find yourself looking out the window in judgment of others, turn back to the mirror and see who you are. You'll find the mirror has a memory. It can remind you of who you once were. That revelation will surely end all judging and fill you with compassion for the ones on the other side of the window.

# 32

# A Prayer Warrior

*When you pray, do not be like the hypocrites,
for they love to pray standing in the synagogues
and on the street corners to be seen by others.
Truly I tell you, they have received their
reward in full. But when you pray, go into
your room, close the door and pray to your
Father, who is unseen. Then your Father, who
sees what is done in secret, will reward you.
And when you pray, do not keep on babbling
like pagans, for they think they will be heard
because of their many words. Do not be like
them, for your Father knows what you need
before you ask him* (Matthew 6:5-8 NIV).

Jesus said that real prayer, attention-getting prayer, God-honoring prayer, heaven-satisfying prayer is not just prayed secretly but prayed sincerely.

Jesus adds that your Father rewards what is done in secret. He's saying secrecy fosters sincerity. God knows that when you take the time to go to a secret place and get alone with him, you are sincere about what you are doing. When you are in that secret place, there is no applause and nobody is clapping for your religious performance, for how skillful you are in talking to God...Do you have that secret place? Do you have that place designated where you can be alone with God?

It can be anywhere. It can be your closet, your basement, your spare bedroom, but you need to have a place of rendezvous where you go and show you mean business with God.

*52 Weeks with Jesus*

━━━━

P rayer is hard for most of us. The moment we begin, a thousand stray thoughts come our way. I wonder what's for dinner tonight? Did I pay the phone bill? When is that dentist appointment? Not today, I hope!

Once we settle down to actually pray, we likely start in with our wants. So-and-so is having medical tests. My brother needs a job. My daughter has an exam today. Oh, the missionary to Peru asked for prayer. And then there's...

And on we go. But Jesus taught us first to acknowledge "our Father in heaven" by "hallowing" his name and offering worship and praise (Matthew 6:9).

Prayer, in God's mind, is about relationship. We are communing with our Creator, and he is communicating with us. Intimate communications are best done in secret.

Pull away to a secret place today. Worship your Lord. Put your "want list" on the back burner. There will be time for that. First, pray by simply being alone with God.

## 33

# Focused on the Father

*[Our Father in heaven…] your will be done, on earth as it is in heaven* (Matthew 6:10 NIV).

———

When you surrender your will to his will, you find that prayer changes you. Your prayers will change as well. That is why getting into that secret place every day and surrendering your will to his is so important. Don't ever leave the place of prayer until you are fully surrendered to Jesus Christ. Without surrender, nothing will change in your life. Nothing will change the perspective of your life. Nothing will change the purpose of your life. Nothing will change the priority of your life like completely being surrendered to his will.

*52 Weeks with Jesus*

———

When the disciples asked Jesus to teach them to pray, I wonder if they knew what they were in for. I can imagine they thought they would learn some surefire way to get what they wanted from God. (Hmmm...that sounds uncomfortably familiar.) Little did they know that in learning how to pray, they would actually be learning about surrendering to God. When praying, we give him *everything*—our worship, our pain, our desires, our fears, our hopes, our dreams. In prayer, we lay them all at the feet of our heavenly Father.

Think of prayer that way today—as a fresh way of absolute surrender. Say along with Jesus in the garden of Gethsemane, "Nevertheless, not as I will, but as you will" (Matthew 26:39). We can pray that way because we know that God's will—God's decisions—are always the best decisions.

# 34

# The One Who Provides

*[Jesus said,] "This, then, is how you should pray"* (Matthew 6:9 NIV).

————

Philip Yancey writes, "We pray because we just can't help but pray."

We pray because we have problems that only God can solve, questions that only God can answer, and needs that only God can meet. That is why we do need to learn how to open up to God in our prayer life.

And as we learn *from Jesus* how to pray, we have the confidence that God *hears* our prayers. He hears me as I pray for you, and he hears you as you pray for me...

We have to go to God, acknowledge our needs, and ask God to meet those needs. When you pray,

you let God do the fighting. Prayer is not just for
defense. Prayer is for offense.

*52 Weeks with Jesus*

⟶

When we have needs, what do we do? *We pray.* Do
you suppose that's exactly *why* God designed
us to have needs—so that we would bond with
him? Seriously, how many people would give prayer a place
in their lives if they had no needs? For that reason, needs are
important to us. The needier we are, the more prayerful we
are—and the more opportunities God has to show his faith-
fulness to us.

Let's praise God in prayer. Let's hallow his name. Let's
surrender to him all our heart desires. And, yes, let's make
our needs known. God knows them, but he instructs us to
ask for his help. Let's allow our neediness to produce the
desired result—driving us to our knees before our caring
Father.

# 35

# The Treasure Principle

*Do not lay up for yourselves treasures on earth, where moth and rust destroy and where thieves break in and steal, but lay up for yourselves treasures in heaven, where neither moth nor rust destroys and where thieves do not break in and steal. For where your treasure is, there your heart will be also.*

*The eye is the lamp of the body. So, if your eye is healthy, your whole body will be full of light, but if your eye is bad, your whole body will be full of darkness. If then the light in you is darkness, how great is the darkness!*

*No one can serve two masters, for either he will hate the one and love the other, or he will be devoted to the one and despise the other. You cannot serve God and money* (Matthew 6:19-24).

One of two things is going to happen to everything that you think you own today, everything that you think is your stuff: you are either going to lose it while you are alive or you are going to leave it once you are dead. That is why Jesus taught what I call the "Treasure Principle," found in Matthew 6:19-24.

The Treasure Principle is not so much about giving your money as managing it. There is far more in the Bible about managing your money than giving your money. The Treasure Principle comes directly from the lips of Jesus and is probably the most brilliant financial advice you will ever be given: you cannot manage your money until you master your money...[But once you know] how to apply it in your life, you will experience real financial freedom and a joy in your life like you never have before.

*52 Weeks with Jesus*

---

Who wouldn't want to live in financial freedom? We all want to, of course, and Jesus gives us the formula. First, we need to realize that we really own nothing. Not our house, not our car, not our rare book collection, not the gold Krugerrands hidden in the box under the bed. All these things—along with our other possessions—came from and ultimately belong to God. Our attitude, then, needs to be one of holding our assets with very loose fingers, knowing that no possession will follow us into heaven. What *does* go to heaven, however, are the treasures we've laid up for that exact purpose. The treasures we experience by giving, not taking; by serving, not being served, by loving, not by disliking or hating.

Heavenly treasures can't be seen on this earth. They are already awaiting us in heaven! Why not make a deposit into your heavenly account today?

# 36

# A Marriage Counselor

*"Haven't you read," [Jesus] replied, "that at the beginning the Creator 'made them male and female,' and said, 'For this reason a man will leave his father and mother and be united to his wife, and the two will become one flesh'? So they are no longer two, but one flesh. Therefore what God has joined together, let no one separate"* (Matthew 19:4-6 NIV).

Do you ever feel like you are stuck with the person you are married to? You are! Getting married and becoming one flesh is not what two people do for each other or even to each other, but what God does for and to them.

Marriage is not what culture joins together. It is not what nature joins together or what the law joins together or what sex joins together or even what love joins together. Marriage is what God joins together.

What has been done by God cannot be undone by humanity. Marriage is always the work of God; divorce is always the work of people—and only God has the right to separate what he has joined together. The good news is that, as the two who've become one look to the One who invented marriage, what God has joined together, God can keep together.

*52 Weeks with Jesus*

When the apostle Paul addressed the sexual immorality within the Corinthian church, he referenced the words in Genesis where God instituted marriage (and were repeated by Jesus): "The two will become one flesh" (1 Corinthians 6:16). But then Paul goes on to add this interesting observation: "But he who is joined to the Lord becomes one spirit with him."

When we became Christians, it was as if we entered into a marriage relationship. God first loved us, then sought us out, then wooed us to himself—and we became his forever. We became glued, as it were, to God. Would we ever dream of severing that relationship with him? *No!* So too God has designed earthly marriage as a picture of our relationship with him. We must not divide what God has united. If we're married, we are to treasure our spouses, to see them as part of ourselves, and to view our marriages as a picture of our permanent union with God.

## 37

# Can One Become Two?

*[Jesus] said to them, "Because of your
hardness of heart Moses allowed you to
divorce your wives, but from the beginning
it was not so"* (Matthew 19:8).

Whenever a ship's captain was heading into a battle where surrender was not an option, he would order that the "colors" be nailed to the mast. Having the flags nailed up high, there was no possibility of lowering them in the heat of the battle in order to surrender. When you go into a battle knowing surrender is not an option, then your only motivation is to fix your mind on how you can best win that battle.

If you are married, nail the flag of your marriage to the post of God's Word and God's will for your life. Remember, your battle is not with your mate—it is for your marriage. Focus your heart and your mind, not on how you can get out of your marriage, but how you can stay true to your "I do" for the glory of God.

*52 Weeks with Jesus*

———

Marriage is from God; divorce is from man and due to the hardness of humanity's heart. A hard heart is a difficult obstacle for any relationship. So what about the times when our hearts are hardened toward God? Our fellowship with our heavenly Father is disturbed whenever we say "no" to him or when we doubt his decisions are for our best.

If a hard heart is the problem—in marriage or in our relationship with God—what can we do? First, we must be willing to acknowledge God's overwhelming love for us *and* demonstrate that by trusting *fully* in all he does. Second, in a Christian marriage relationship, though the two have become one, there is always a third person. That Person is God. He united you as a couple, and he doesn't leave you to fend for yourselves. God plans to be part of your marriage always.

If even one partner in a difficult marriage will include God as part of the relationship, it will soften that partner's heart...and possibly the difficult partner's as well.

# 38

# Love: Can Two Stay One?

*A new commandment I give to you, that you love one another: just as I have loved you, you also are to love one another. By this all people will know that you are my disciples, if you have love for one another* (John 13:34-35).

Tucked away in a Gospel is a little two-paragraph statement Jesus made that gives us the foundation for any enduring relationship. It speaks of the kind of love that is so strong that if a husband and wife have it, nothing can break it.

Jesus wasn't even talking about marriage when he said this. He wasn't talking to spouses; he was talking to disciples. What Jesus said to believers, generally, I am going to apply to marriage specifically.

*52 Weeks with Jesus*

When our marriages include God as the third partner, he becomes our model for love. The two-paragraph statement that is foundational for marriage or any other enduring relationship is summed up as loving one another just as Jesus loves us. So how committed is Jesus's love to us? That's easily answered by looking at the cross. Jesus's commitment to us was to the death...a painful death. He gave his all. And that's the model for enduring love. Bottom line? *You stay in love with love from above.*

# 39

# The Number One Priority

*Seek first the kingdom of God and his righteousness, and all these things will be added to you* (Matthew 6:33).

━━━━

If my number one priority in life is to seek God's kingdom and God's righteousness, then everything I do can be ordered by two things. Where I work, how I spend my time, the person I marry, how I manage my money, what I buy always have to be sifted and sorted through one filter: "Is this for his kingdom? Does it relate to his righteousness?"

*52 Weeks with Jesus*

━━━━

In our world, Jesus's recipe for success sounds radical, doesn't it? Implicit in first seeking the kingdom of God and his righteousness is that we *don't* seek first a career, a family, money, fame, position, worldly security—all the things our neighbors seem to be pursuing. The question, then, for our neighbors is, "What assurance do you have that the things you're so eager to pursue will bring you contentment?" Stories abound of those who achieved material success but died sad and broken.

On the other hand, God offers assurance to those who pursue him and his righteousness as their first priority. The assurance is that all else that we need will be provided. Centuries before Christ spoke that assurance, his earthly forebearer said the same thing. David wrote, "The young lions suffer want and hunger; but those who seek the LORD lack no good thing" (Psalm 34:10). There is no down side to seeking God and his righteousness first. There is only the promise of lacking no good thing.

## Section 6

# Jesus, the Helper

———

One of Jesus's most endearing qualities was the way he proactively pursued the outcast and outsider. He was a man of the people, not just the privileged. He was a master for the masses, not a rabbi for the rich. Jesus sought out those who society avoided, mocked, and ridiculed. He was willing to help anyone at any time—even if they didn't realize they needed him. Jesus's most scandalous encounters reveal his role as a helper of the helpless and the hope of the hopeless, all the while changing the way we see others and ourselves.

*52 Weeks with Jesus*

# 40

# The Thirst Quencher

*The Samaritan woman said to him, "You are a Jew and I am a Samaritan woman. How can you ask me for a drink?" (For Jews do not associate with Samaritans.)*

*Jesus answered her, "If you knew the gift of God and who it is that asks you for a drink, you would have asked him and he would have given you living water"* (John 4:9-10 NIV).

Jesus is sitting on top of the well. As a man, he was expected to withdraw to a distance of at least twenty feet, indicating it was both safe and appropriate for her to come to the well. But Jesus doesn't move. He is waiting to meet her.

In that day, a man, particularly a stranger, not only would not talk to a woman, but he wouldn't even make eye contact with her. Not only does Jesus break the sexual barrier when he speaks to her, he breaks the racial barrier. He ignores a seven-hundred-year hostility that had been going on between Jews and Samaritans.

The woman is shocked and thinks, Are you blind? Not only am I a woman, but I am also a Samaritan!

And that's just the point. Jesus chose this time, this place, and this woman to have one of the greatest conversations he would ever have.

And just as he waited for this woman, he is waiting to meet us. Jesus is not the least bit bothered by who you are, what you've done, or what anybody else thinks of you.

*52 Weeks with Jesus*

⸻

In this, the longest of Jesus's conversations recorded in Scripture, we find him talking to a Samaritan woman—an outcast. The subject of her "mess ups" came up. She had five husbands—and the man she was currently with wasn't her husband. Does Jesus chide her for her sins? Oddly, he does just the opposite. He takes advantage of the fact that she's drawing water from the well and offers her "living water." And what must she do to obtain this living water? Simply *ask*.

Have you had a recent conversation with Jesus about your mess ups…your sins? Have you been burdened by the things you've done that you shouldn't have? Have you felt remorse over the things you haven't done that you should have? The great thing about such conversations with Jesus is that, as with the woman at the well, they result in an invitation from him. That invitation isn't to try harder next time or to beat yourself up over your sins. Nor must you have a priest or anyone else intercede for you. No, the invitation is far simpler: *Ask Jesus for living water.*

Jesus's well never runs dry, no matter how often we come to him with our failures and regrets.

## 41

# A Most Valuable Treasure

*As Jesus started on his way, a man ran up to him and fell on his knees before him. "Good teacher," he asked, "what must I do to inherit eternal life?"*

*"Why do you call me good?" Jesus answered. "No one is good—except God alone. You know the commandments: 'You shall not murder, you shall not commit adultery, you shall not steal, you shall not give false testimony, you shall not defraud, honor your father and mother.'"*

*"Teacher," he declared, "all these I have kept since I was a boy."*

*Jesus looked at him and loved him. "One thing you lack," he said. "Go, sell everything you have and give to the poor, and you will have treasure in heaven. Then come, follow me."*

*At this the man's face fell. He went away sad, because he had great wealth* (Mark 10:17-22 NIV).

After Christian fighters captured Jerusalem during the First Crusade, pilgrims from all over Western Europe began visiting the Holy Land. Around AD 1100, a French knight formed an organization called the Knights Templar. Their job was to protect these pilgrims during their visit. When these knights were baptized by the church, they brought their swords with them. But the knights didn't take their swords under water with them. Instead, they held their swords up out of the water while they were immersed. They were saying to Jesus, "You can have control of all of me, except this one part. I am all yours, except when I am on the battlefield. All that I have is yours, except this sword."

When people today get baptized they don't hold up a sword, but they hold up their wallets. Their laptops. Deeds to their homes. Their 401(k)s. They hold up their pride, their egos, their bitterness, their grudges.

Only when you surrender everything to Jesus can you avoid becoming the biggest loser and let him transform you into the biggest winner.

*52 Weeks with Jesus*

The men of the Knights Templar who were baptized holding their swords above water had much in common with the rich young ruler. The knights were obeying God...up to a point. The rich young ruler would do anything to inherit eternal life...up to a point. That point, in both cases, revealed what truly had captured their hearts. That one thing that simply could not be surrendered..._would_ not be surrendered.

The question for us today is whether we have this in common with the rich young ruler and the members of the Knights Templar. Are we willing to give all to Jesus...up to a point? What do we know in the secret part of our hearts that we don't want God to have? Our reputations? (Are we embarrassed to be followers of Jesus?) Our talents? ("But, God, the secular world is where my talents belong...it's where they'll be noticed.") Our ambitions? ("God, I promise when I'm promoted to president of the company I'll give you the glory.") Our passions? (Oh, Lord, please don't ask me to go _there_!)

The irony is that God wants to add to our lives, not subtract from them. The things we're called to surrender are the very things that impede our progress in his kingdom. When we surrender all, we win all. What we try to keep, we eventually lose.

# 42

# A Gracious Judge

*Those who heard began to go away one at a time, the older ones first, until only Jesus was left, with the woman still standing there. Jesus straightened up and asked her, "Woman, where are they? Has no one condemned you?"*

*"No one, sir," she said.*

*"Then neither do I condemn you," Jesus declared. "Go now and leave your life of sin"* (John 8:9-11 NIV).

Condemning sin is not the same as judging the sinner. Jesus said two things to this woman, and they both go together: "Woman, I don't condemn you, but I do condemn what you did. Go and do it no more."

Jesus loves us just the way we are, but he loves us too much to let us stay that way. Condemning sinners is not my job or yours. But condemning sin is.

Jesus gives us grace and removes our guilt so he can lead us to goodness. When this woman encountered Jesus, when she received grace and repented of her sin, her brokenness was turned into blessing. And you're invited to let Jesus do the same for you.

*52 Weeks with Jesus*

Sometimes we forget that sin is a destructive force in our lives. When we engage in it, we may not feel the repercussions immediately. However, there are *always* consequences to sin.

One consequence is that we become susceptible to the deceitfulness of sin. We engage in a sin, and the next time we find it easier to do so. We become "softened" toward sin.

Continuing in sin results in further deception. Few people caught up in a sinful addiction were addicted the first time out. The repeated behavior—the repeated choosing the same way of acting out—eventually takes its toll.

God extends grace to us in our sins—but he loves us too much to let us remain deceived and addicted. When he tells us to "go now and leave your life of sin," he's leading us back to goodness, wholeness, and a clear conscience.

Our brokenness, like the woman's caught in adultery, can be turned into blessings. The sweetest words someone caught in sin can hear are surely, "Neither do I condemn you...Go now and leave your life of sin."

# 43

# Always Available, Always Accessible

*There was a woman who had had a discharge of blood for twelve years, and who had suffered much under many physicians, and had spent all that she had, and was no better but rather grew worse. She had heard the reports about Jesus and came up behind him in the crowd and touched his garment. For she said, "If I touch even his garments, I will be made well." And immediately the flow of blood dried up, and she felt in her body that she was healed of her disease* (Mark 5:25-29).

Leo Tolstoy, the great Russian writer, tells of the time he was walking down the street and passed a beggar. He reached into his pocket to get the beggar some money, but his pocket was empty. He felt bad. Rather than just ignore the man and keep walking, he turned to the man and said, "I am so sorry, my brother, that I don't have anything to give you." The beggar's face widened into a smile the size of a half moon. He said, "Mister, you have given me more than I could have ever asked for: you have called me 'brother.'"

You and I are called to do the same, to minister the grace, the love, and the power of Jesus Christ—to be the hem of his garment.

*52 Weeks with Jesus*

People touch us every day. Not literally, perhaps, but figuratively. Every time we interact with a store clerk, a business associate, a family member, or even a stranger, we're engaging in a touch of sorts. Most of the time the touch is no more than that. "Have a good day," is perhaps the climax of most of our interactions. But could it be that way because we expect no more than that? What might happen if we took the time to allow God to work through us as we touch people throughout the day? What if we said to someone, "How may I pray for you today?" Or instead of a casual glance, what if we took the time to read another person's demeanor? Their sadness or happiness will show in their faces...if we only take the time to perceive it.

God may set up divine encounters when we can demonstrate his love by a simple verbal touch that shows we care. "Touching" people is an enormous blessing for us as well as for the person whom we've touched with Jesus's love. Let's pray for more opportunities to genuinely touch others.

# 44

# Our Best Friend

*Jesus entered Jericho and was passing through. A man was there by the name of Zacchaeus; he was a chief tax collector and was wealthy. He wanted to see who Jesus was, but because he was short he could not see over the crowd. So he ran ahead and climbed a sycamore-fig tree to see him, since Jesus was coming that way.*

*When Jesus reached the spot, he looked up and said to him, "Zacchaeus, come down immediately. I must stay at your house today." So he came down at once and welcomed him gladly.*

*All the people saw this and began to mutter, "He has gone to be the guest of a sinner"* (Luke 19:1-7 NIV).

Why was [Zacchaeus] so determined? Maybe because Jesus had developed quite the reputation.

People were calling him a glutton and a drunkard, a friend of tax collectors and sinners. People who felt unloved by everybody else felt loved by Jesus.

The more those who are not followers of Christ are loved by those of us who are followers of Christ, the more open they may be to following Christ. Specifically, we should be attractive to them by the way we love them, by the way we respect them, and by the way we treat them.

*52 Weeks with Jesus*

———

It's easy to love the lovely. Not so much the unlovely, and even less so the ugly. To his contemporaries, Zacchaeus was ugly. He was a chief tax collector, a thief, a traitor. Despised by all. And then Jesus came along. Jesus who not only noticed Zacchaeus, but sought him out. "Come down from that tree, Zeke! I want to have dinner with you tonight." Can you imagine Zacchaeus's reaction? Actually, we don't have to imagine it. We're told that meeting Jesus so changed Zacchaeus that he declared, "Behold, Lord, the half of my goods I give to the poor. And if I have defrauded anyone of anything, I restore it fourfold." Jesus then remarked, "Today salvation has come to this house, since he also is a son of Abraham. For the Son of Man came to seek and to save the lost."

Are we not also to seek and save the lost by presenting the good news of the gospel? How does this happen if we don't notice people the way Jesus noticed them? Salvation comes when the lost are noticed and loved by the found.

## Section 7

# Jesus, the Leader

———

Few words are batted about by managers, pastors, entrepreneurs, and politicians more than *leadership*. When we want to learn how to lead, we often look to those whose names emblazon book covers and fancy business cards. But what about the leader who claims more followers than any person in history? What made Jesus such a great leader? The answer has the power to transform us into people of influence and impact.

*52 Weeks with Jesus*

# 45

# The Standard of Greatness

*[Jesus said,] "If anyone would be first, he must be last of all and servant of all"* (Mark 9:35).

You want to be number one? Then here is the secret: look for every opportunity you can to be number two. You want to be considered as one of the greatest of all time? Then learn this lesson: greatness starts at the bottom. You want to be like Jesus Christ? Find the least desired position. Find a job nobody else wants to do. Find the worst seat in the house.

*52 Weeks with Jesus*

God's ways are so very different from ours. To us, leadership means commanding others, being looked up to, being considered "the boss." But in God's kingdom, it's just the opposite. To truly lead is to act as a servant. The way up is down. Not only is this counter to our natural way of thinking, it's counter to our very natures. We want to be noticed, not hidden. We want others to see and applaud our efforts. We wrongly tie our self-worth into how well others approve of us, when we really need only be concerned with God's opinion.

We already know our true self-worth is determined by the price God was willing to pay for us—the life of his Son, Jesus Christ. Being firmly grounded in that truth, we can divest ourselves of the opinions of others and get about becoming first by looking for ways to serve others.

## 46

# A Servant First

*[Jesus] got up from the meal, took off his outer
clothing, and wrapped a towel around his waist.
After that, he poured water into a basin and
began to wash his disciples' feet, drying them
with the towel that was wrapped around him.*

*He came to Simon Peter, who said to him,
"Lord, are you going to wash my feet?"*

*Jesus replied, "You do not realize now what I
am doing, but later you will understand."*

*"No," said Peter, "you shall never wash my feet."*

*Jesus answered, "Unless I wash you, you have no
part with me"* (John 13:4-8 NIV).

The good news of the gospel is that once Jesus
bathes you in the waters of his saving grace, you
never need another bath. However, your feet will
get dirty. Once we surrender ourselves to him and

admit we need him to wash us, only then will we see opportunities every day to follow his example and to serve the needs of others.

*52 Weeks with Jesus*

———▸

How often do we go through our days oblivious to the needs of those around us? Most people don't talk about their deepest needs. They don't tell us their worries about their aged parent. They likely won't mention their troubled marriage or their suspicions about their teen's drug use. Their looming financial disaster is likely unknown to us. That is, unless we've previously shown that we regard them as more than just coworkers or neighbors or customers. When we do the unexpected, when we do the twenty-first-century equivalent of washing their feet, we open a bridge between us that makes it easier to cross back and forth—us to them and them to us.

The truth is, many people pray about the needs of the people they know. But when God sends a person to help meet that need, our friends are able to see God's love in action. The Bible they may not read, but they do read us as believers in Christ. We represent God when we meet the needs of the people around us.

Washing the feet of another is dirty work. We have to step out of our comfort zones. But that's where God is, and that's where he wants us. God's calling is to the front lines of the battle instead of hanging out in the canteen for cookies and punch.

# 47

# The Victor

*Jesus was led up by the Spirit into the wilderness to be tempted by the devil* (Matthew 4:1).

Jesus had two secret weapons to fight temptation. And they're the same ones we have. Jesus was filled with the Spirit, and he was armed with the Scriptures.

Jesus was led by the Holy Spirit of God. He was, and we are, led only as we follow. We follow someone only if we are totally surrendered and submitted to their authority. We surrender our lives to the Holy Spirit because he is God's nuclear weapon that will enable us to defeat temptation.

Jesus Christ was also armed with the Scriptures. Jesus never tried to argue with the devil; he didn't try to negotiate with the devil; he never tried to debate with the devil. He didn't use magic formulas or magic words. He didn't use holy water or anointed handkerchiefs. He used the Word of God.

*52 Weeks with Jesus*

ow are you doing in your ongoing battle with temptation? Oh yes, I know you're tempted—perhaps even daily. Perhaps several times a day. If you're alive and breathing, you're a tempted person. Temptation is normal and to be expected. God knows all about our weaknesses, about those areas where we're particularly susceptible to the lures of the enemy. He never expects us to go into battle unarmed. In fact, if we could really see the battle from God's point of view, we'd breathe a sigh of relief at the armor available to us through the powerful promises in God's Word and the might of the Holy Spirit dwelling in us.

During your next severe temptation, don't place confidence in your human ability to resist. You'll fail every time. Instead, nuke the enemy's lies the way Jesus did. Through the promises in the Word and being led of the Holy Spirit, Jesus prevailed through far worse temptations than yours and mine. We can trust him for our weapons and protection. He blazed the trail to victory over temptation.

# 48

# Commander in Chief

*[Jesus said,] "If anyone would come after me,
let him deny himself and take up his cross
daily and follow me. For whoever would save
his life will lose it, but whoever loses his life
for my sake will save it"* (Luke 9:23-24).

＞＞＞＞

One Sunday I surprised my congregation by announcing, publicly, the church member who was giving me the most problems. Seriously, this guy was my biggest headache. I wasn't sure if I should say his name out loud because—at one level—I liked the guy. I loved being around him, and he's one of the best people I know. With a bit of fear and trepidation, I said aloud that the church member who was giving me the most trouble was...me! I have to constantly tell myself to get out of the way so Jesus can have his way.

Jesus said, "If you are going to follow me, step one is to deny yourself." That means you have to put Jesus before you, above you, ahead of you, and instead of you. You've got to get the makeup of your life to be all of Jesus and none of you.

*52 Weeks with Jesus*

---

enying one's self doesn't sound like much fun, frankly. Like any gamble, it involves an unknown outcome. What will happen to me if I truly deny myself to follow Jesus? But wait. There *is* an expected outcome after all—both for those who choose to deny themselves for the sake of Christ and for those who don't. The promised outcome for those who won't deny themselves is loss ("whoever would save his life will lose it"), while the promised outcome for those who deny themselves to follow Christ is that they will save their lives ("whoever loses his life for my sake will save it").

Really, isn't losing our life to find it in Christ the surest bet of all?

# Jesus, the Overcomer

›‒‒‒‒‒

What separates Jesus from every other human and religious figure in history was not what he did *during* his life but what he accomplished in his final hours. More than his miracles or parables, teachings or maxims, Jesus is defined by the way he overcame death for the sake of humankind. In Jesus's last days, he overcame the three greatest problems of life—sin, sorrow, and death—and through this, he gives us hope that we can also be victorious when our life's final chapter has been written.

*52 Weeks with Jesus*

# 49

# The Passion of Christ—
# The Rest of the Story

*While we were still weak, at the right time
Christ died for the ungodly. For one will scarcely
die for a righteous person—though perhaps for
a good person one would dare even to die—but
God shows his love for us in that while we were
still sinners, Christ died for us* (Romans 5:6-8).

Jesus took on the cross what you will have to take
for all eternity if you don't take Jesus. He died such
a violent death to illustrate how horrible sin is, how
holy God is, and how much we need him to die in
our place for our sins.

*52 Weeks with Jesus*

These days it seems like much of sin is getting a pass. In fact, "sin" is hardly considered sin anymore. What used to be spoken of in hushed tones is now broadcast into millions of homes every night. What was once decried as ruinous to a person's life is now celebrated as yet another option. If John Newton was writing "Amazing Grace" today, he'd have naysayers suggesting he change that line about grace saving "a wretch like me."

A *wretch*? The truth is, sin has lost its wretchedness reputation. It has been dumbed down to accommodate those who find pleasure in it. And yet—and this is the tragedy—sin hasn't lost one ounce of its power to destroy lives. Daily we see the devastation of sin, though few are willing to acknowledge it these days.

The good news is that, although sin is still as destructive as ever, the cross is as powerful as ever. Nothing can diminish what Jesus did at Calvary for us. We have at our disposal an antidote to the sin in our lives and the sin in our culture.

Though you've sinned as have I, we can take comfort in the resolute fact that the penalty for our sins has been fully paid. "Amazing grace" is truly Christ, the godly, dying for you and me, the ungodly.

## 50

# His Grace, My Place

*The chief priests and the elders persuaded the crowd to ask for Barabbas and to have Jesus executed.*

*"Which of the two do you want me to release to you?" asked the governor.*

*"Barabbas," they answered.*

*"What shall I do, then, with Jesus who is called the Messiah?" Pilate asked.*

*They all answered, "Crucify him!"*

*"Why? What crime has he committed?" asked Pilate.*

*But they shouted all the louder, "Crucify him!"* (Matthew 27:20-23 NIV).

When the crowd at Jesus's crucifixion was given the choice to release one prisoner—as was the local custom—they chose a notorious prisoner named Barabbas over Jesus.

Barabbas was Osama bin Laden and Saddam Hussein rolled into one. He was a murderer, a robber, a rebel, and a thief who'd been convicted more than once, and he expected that this was the day he was going to die. I imagine that when he was set free from that prison, he wandered over to that place where he was supposed to be hanging. Maybe he even stood at the foot of that cross and mused, "I don't know who you are, but one thing I do know—you are dying in my place."

*We are all Barabbas.*

Jesus was not only Barabbas's substitute, he was our substitute. He not only died in his place, he died in our place. Paul later explains to the church in Galatia, "Christ...changed places with us and put himself under that curse" (Galatians 3:13 NCV).

*52 Weeks with Jesus*

Sometimes it's hard for us to think of ourselves as sinners—as Barabbas. "I'm not so bad," we say. "Actually, compared to most people, I'm probably above average in terms of being good." Have you ever thought that? If yes, I have a suggestion. The next time you wonder if you're really such a sinner, pray the most dangerous prayer of all: "Lord, show me my sinfulness." The full impact of what happened on the cross is reserved for those who have come face-to-face with their own depravity. It's then that we see the true need for our Savior. For someone who will take our place because we know we dare not face God alone without an Advocate.

If you have doubts about your sinfulness, pray the prayer...and wait and watch. If you have no doubts about your bankrupt state before God, rejoice. God has given all to save you! He has exchanged your bankruptcy for his riches through the death and resurrection of his Son.

## 51

# The Warrior Rises

*When the centurion and those who were with him, keeping watch over Jesus, saw the earthquake and what took place, they were filled with awe and said, "Truly this was the Son of God!"* (Matthew 27:54).

When you understand why Jesus died on the cross and what happened after his death on the cross, then you understand why only he could be the warrior who could give every one of us the ability to win our war over the two greatest problems this world faces: sin and death. Jesus is the only warrior who could defeat and who did defeat sin and death...

Sin was an enemy too big for anybody to fight. It was a war too great for anybody to win—until the warrior came. This warrior used the only weapon that could defeat sin and death and bruise the devil, who caused it all. Though the people did not realize it yet, that weapon was not a sword or a spear or an arrow. It was a cross. This warrior performed the ultimate act any soldier can: he gave his life for the freedom of others.

*52 Weeks with Jesus*

T he people of Israel were looking for a warrior to save them. It's no surprise, then, that when the promised Messiah came in the form of a lowly carpenter with no military credentials, they didn't recognize him. And yet Jesus was a warrior after all. He took on the grandest battles in history and won. Can you think of more terrifying foes than sin and death? That's what Christ triumphed over. That's the battle he won *for us*!

Our response needs to be remembering that from his death came true life for us: eternal life in the future and a redeemed, victorious life here and now. The greatest warrior ("Truly, this was the Son of God!") won the greatest battles and gave us the greatest spoils.

# 52

# Dead Man Walking

*Jesus said to [Martha], "I am the resurrection
and the life. Whoever believes in me, though
he die, yet shall he live, and everyone who
lives and believes in me shall never die.
Do you believe this?"* (John 11:25-26).

Everyone needs hope.

We need hope that our life matters today, but we also need hope that there is more to life than this life tomorrow. Everybody wants to know that they matter. We want to know that our life makes a difference here on earth and that somehow life continues after our journey on earth is over.

Every human being on this planet longs for significance and security. Nobody knows that better than the God who made us, which is why he sent Jesus...

The One who performed that unforgettable miracle on Lazarus later went to the cross, hung there, and died, paying the complete penalty for your sin and mine. He too was wrapped in burial cloths. He too was placed in the grave. He too was sealed with a stone. But three days later he was alive, never to die again.

We must answer Jesus's query to Martha: Do you believe this?

I hope you do because there's nobody like Jesus. Never has been. Never will be.

*52 Weeks with Jesus*

▸▸▸▸

Our God is the God of hope when we feel there is no hope. He's the God of life in the midst of death. He's the God of love when we seem surrounded by hate. He's the God of restoration when there seems to be only destruction. He's the God of forgiveness when there is transgression.

When Lazarus was sick, Martha expected Jesus to come and heal him. But Jesus didn't do that. He let Martha's hope run out as Lazarus died. And then Jesus brought life out of death, hope out of hopelessness, health out of sickness.

Jesus still does it all for us. Sometimes, like Martha, we expect God to bring us hope as we envision it. That's not always the way he works though. But in all cases of hope-lessness, if we look to him, he *will* give us hope—hope that extends beyond this life. We need only to answer Jesus's question to Martha in the affirmative: "Do you believe this?" I pray your answer is "Yes!" because there's nobody like Jesus. Never has been. Never will be.

If you enjoyed *52 Weeks with Jesus Devotional*, you'll want to read Dr. Merritt's other book on his year-long encounter with Jesus Christ.

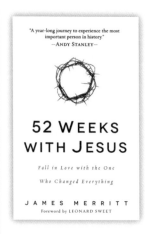

"A year-long journey to experience the most important person in history."
—ANDY STANLEY—

52 WEEKS WITH JESUS

*Fall in Love with the One*
*Who Changed Everything*

JAMES MERRITT
Foreword by LEONARD SWEET

Jesus Christ is the most influential human to ever walk the earth. We've heard and seen so many depictions of him that we think we know him better than we actually do. If we took the time to really look at him, we might be surprised at what we'd find. In *52 Weeks with Jesus*, author and pastor James Merritt leads you on a transformational journey as he shares what he's learned over a lifetime of studying Jesus's life and ministry. As you join Dr. Merritt on this journey, you will come to know and encounter Jesus in new and surprising ways and be inspired anew to embrace his invitation, "Come, follow Me."

Filled with practical applications and surprising truths, this book will help you more ably answer that ancient question that's as timely today as when it was first posed: "Who do you say that I am?"

## About the Author

James Merritt is senior pastor of Cross Pointe Church in Duluth, Georgia, and the host of *Touching Lives,* a television show that broadcasts weekly in all 50 states and 122 countries. He formerly served as a two-term president of the Southern Baptist Convention, America's largest Protestant denomination. As a national voice on faith and leadership, he has been interviewed by *Time, Fox News, ABC World News, MSNBC,* and *60 Minutes.*

He is author of nine books, including *How to Impact and Influence Others: 9 Keys to Successful Leadership*; *What God Wants Every Dad to Know*; and *Still Standing: 8 Winning Strategies for Facing Tough Times.*

Dr. Merritt holds a bachelor's degree from Stetson University and a master's and doctor of philosophy from Southern Baptist Theological Seminary. He and his wife, Teresa, reside outside of Atlanta near their three children and two grandchildren.

Follow him on Twitter at @DrJamesMerritt.

To learn more about Harvest House books and
to read sample chapters, visit our website:

**www.harvesthousepublishers.com**